Diktsamling

Diktsamling

SOFIA HÄLLGREN

Diktsamling

Sättning och omslagsutformning: BoD – Books on Demand

Förlag: BoD – Books on Demand, Stockholm, Sverige

Tryck: BoD – Books on Demand, Norderstedt, Tyskland

ISBN: 978-91-7569-659-1

She's hanging up in strings
blown glass and pearls
and snowflakes in porcelaine.
She's an artist
Her art of some
female ghost in a white dress
and long black hair, with an
angst filled expression, is
on display in an old house
from the 18th century.
She paints and sculpts
and blows glass and
has her art in shortfilms
and her poetry.
She sculpts a naked pregnant
woman and a polarbear
for a East Indian couple
who loves polarbears.
She listens to Vivaldi
piccola flute concert
in her artstudio.
Brushes, a cowskull,
spiderhats, angels
seraphs in jade and
khol. She's beautiful
as a day and has a tshirt
with a black panther and stars.
She's a scenographer who
does art for movie, tv and
theatre.
She's smiling and showing
a coffin with the wing of a bird
and a babydoll with it's eye

poked out.
She films at the cathedral
and the morgue.
Together with some poetry
by EE Cummings to the
dead bodies.

The night
with it's roof
of black as pitch coal
and stars that someone
put up, so they would shine
and everybody would see
them, and hate the sun
(thats on a tarotcard
with the Magician)
and her diamonds glitter
on her military green hippiebag
as a girl on a theatre stage
with garlands of faery light,
trees and vaults and draperies
and clothes from a second hand
shop, does A midsummers nights
dream. She brushes her teeth
infront of her mirror late at night
all alone in her apartment when
the nightingale cries and someone
dies. The fae folk fly around like
fireflies in their world unseen to us
mortals. She's got wings of a faery,
pink and green. And a costume that
makes her look like a faery princess,
a dress that glows and a hat made of
glowing fabric. She's looking up space
in a dictionary and …
Mickey Mouse and Minnie get engaged
and marry.

Poem of Saturns lost glitter shoes

She walks with a pink umbrella
in the space station where humans
have been forced to evacuate since
the world war 4 ruined Mother earth.
She's got pink curly hair and a vinered mascara
she bought at transfer, Babyglitter Alien
from Mars mascara and she's got
„Unicorn" from Nirvanarain lipgloss. Shes gorgeous, purple
lips
and green eyebrows with silverstreaks.
She's wearing contacts that are red.
She's getting married to a man with
a silver streak in his black hair and
superhero clothes that's handsome as
fuck. She misses Paris and the Eiffel tower,
but they've got a mini eiffel tower at the new
world in Mars and an Eiffel tower at
the white with cherry blossom mascara box from French kiss-
ing.
She's got a mini Geisha
purse, a Manga princess Geisha with
red flower petals that fall and the Geisha
is smiling wearing a kimono with
red and white streaks.
Theyvé got special trekkers
who take care of the dead and
dying and they've got clothes
of iron and blue rubber.
She's walking and hits a big
xmas tree that someone's put up
and ow! She hits herself against it.

The planets swing by as the orchestra
plays a tune for mother earth.
She's gorgeous with her fake eyelashes
by Omino Kutoro, It. They make fake eyelashes
with rainbow glitter, lipsticks with rainbow colour,
mascaras and makeup for the new world…
And she takes a candy from her black bag
with a Geisha on it called Japanese moon candy,
a salted licorice. Nirvanarain at the shop looks
like lilac stars in a swirl. The spacestation shop
has French kissing, Nirvanarain, Omino Kutoro It
and Babyglitter Alien from Mars's new mascara.
She's wearing them all.

The like

She's got a basket full of the moon,
she will take it home and put a straw
and drink moonjuice. Stars she takes down
one by one and the black cat helps her.
She puts the stars up in the ninth dimension
and forgets the world. She walks galaxies,
and lives there for months at a time.
She sleeps next to the dying swan.
She believes in the dark god
worshipping him, painting with
a brush of swan feather
on the paper. She is in the
astral realm where her soul flies.
She's in a room in the ninth dimension,
where she's watching TV...
She's got a sixth sense
and speaks to spirits on the
spirit phone. She's beautiful
and wakes up the night
from it's cradlelike sleep
to have beercans dance along the
highway, the lost highway at
night. A couple is sucked into a Ufo
and stay there.

Autumn in new york
Pearls
mother of pearl
hanging from the ceiling
touch them
make sounds
glasses that you play on
whistle blow
makes whistling sounds
your perfume
lingers on
in this room
your spirit
I watch you
strange one
as you move slowly across the room
smiling
laughing
it's autumn
leaves falling
dancing through liquid air
your hands touches the outer layers
whilst your eyes talk not mundane
but air
living breathing air
and your white hands dance
it's autumn in New York
and you've got this year to live
the heart
tells nothing and it hurts
(I know)
ophelia
to see everything

atoms
molecules
the street
to fill up to the brim
with death
the tumor washes away life
to find nothing underneath
but a wasting flower
about to die
but that can't last forever, can it?
Snow falls over new york
it tumbles down seeking comfort
you speak naught but tumble away
into vast dimensions
beyond the wall of sleep
to last forever
but forever is a lie
now you're a story I tell to women
everywhere
the hats linger on
go on without a care
mother of pearl dances in the breeze
autumn in New york
sad not bad
to see your enigma
wash away with the sun

The like
a girl with short black hair
walks the space holding a white umbrella.
She's smiling and laughing and
jumping from galaxies and
planets. She's smoking
funny, and talks to the
halfmoon. Stars she takes
home with her in her house.
She puts them up on the ceiling
and puts on the light. She
lights candles and look at her
artwork that begins to live
its' own life. She's astral
projecting and does herbal
witchcraft and plays with her
wand, a crystal one, pink.
Her house that's in space,
is white with a pool.
Shes sewing an alien
shirt because she needs
it for her neighbour.
She's gothic and
believes in the
Gods of the old
Celts.
She does a ritual with
her wand and has a pentagram
made of gothic clouds and wool.
She owns a Cerberos and a
turtle and has a computer

The like
she is
drinking from the stars
starwater. The like is.
Milk from the cow in universe
which Romulus and Remus
drink from when they're (in jade) finished with the wolf.
Universe puts up a scarf with batique blue and green.
She goes to the artshop and buys a pad to paint on
and a brush of stardust and hair from a unicorn.
She's got an astral child with a man she loves.
Astral love, astral funerals in the astral sphere.
She is heartbroken and afraid. She burns candles
in the cathedrals basement, holding a skull wearing
a monkrobe. She is Robin hoods relative and
knows how to burn sage infront of frightened
people who live in the haunted apartment.
Shoes of an angel with stars and dust.

The like

She's got a basket full of the moon,
she will take it home and put a straw
and drink moonjuice. Stars she takes down
one by one and the black cat helps her.
She puts the stars up in the ninth dimension
and forgets the world. She walks galaxies,
and lives there for months at a time.
She sleeps next to the dying swan.
She believes in the dark god
worshipping him, painting with
a brush of swan feather
on the paper. She is in the
astral realm where her soul flies.
She's in a room in the ninth dimension,
where she's watching TV...
She's got a sixth sense
and speaks to spirits on the
spirit phone. She's beautiful
and wakes up the night
from it's cradlelike sleep
to have beercans dance along the
highway, the lost highway at
night. A couple is sucked into a Ufo
and stay there.

The like
ghosts of
luxurious opera singers
and the lawyers
put away.
She is.
A skyscraper
and an architect.
She steals blobs
of slime in the Halloween
shop and fangs.
The like since they're all
dead and gone now.
She's waiting for
me, and worm
eaten is the apple
the nymph holds
in the renaissance
painting. She's worth
gold for him.
Glass heart and glass slipper,
is what's left of Cinderella.
She's tender towards the
extinct dront. She's got
My little ponies that have
rainbow tail and mane,
white, with yellow stars.
I.
Weep for the I.
I do.

Skulls

I
Ghosttown
anonymous ghosts
cry here
wavering
their premonitions
they aren't here
for laughs
they're here for breaking
the gates
from where deaths cold jaws clutched them
needless to say afraid of

everything and everyone
ghosts sitting in lonely rooms
saloons
drinking whiskey that goes right through them
combing their hair
smiling skulls
ageing never

II
some of them
outlaws
dont'know they're dead
not understanding why modern dressed gents
show themselves in their saloons
gun in hand they stand face to face with their victims
while people walk around
eyewitnesses to past tragedies
history gunfights

death sneaking it's quiet way around
these ol gunfighters

outlaws till death
they scream
but no one can hear them
ghosts dead
undead

outside, a wind rustles through town
stir up cactusflowers
a skull of a cow
blue clear sky
this is where the ghosts rule
night after night they buckle up
night after night, a wind goes through cold faces
who know they're dead over and over again
skeletons skulls death
they grin

and fight till death forever

Nature

Windchimes
through them I can see
trees, leaves,
falling snowflakes,
life, sunshine
your smile
left bare
at the hands of nature

Apache

ghost
desert
desertflower
traveling through veins
numbing the mind
rites
passages through poets brain
great endymion named night
ghost of dead indian in head
heyo heyo heyo heyo
i'm lost
peyote the sun
the son and the road
cold night
in desert

Keats

Keats näktergal
sjunger på morgonen
enhörningen smiter iväg
huset på Hampstead Heath
dödsrikets diktarsjälar
Song of the Indian maid
Ode on Melancholy
innan hjärnans myller samlats
var du rädd att dö
du skrev Ode on a Grecian urn
och To Autumn
i en feberrik yrsel
Lille John och Robin modig
Robin Hood
och dödstankar
trappan i Rom
Lethe
drömlik blick
död vid 25

Dikt
Spöken av neurosedynbarn
din älskares inälvor
din sperma i en kopp
Kafkas tredje hjärna
dina ögon betraktande
en tavla av Kafka
och ett lik
jag ler i mjugg
inför din person
vampyr
ensambarn
hemsöker du mig
återigen vid mitt fönster

Chinese woman
The chinese woman with her funerals
and her food grooving her time in
halfwitted chapels
dimlit by neon lights
her dead speak to her

rice falls from the sky.

Garden
Garden with incense
and stones
and candles
burning bright
in the night
there, they worship
death and burn fires
and draw with charcoal on
naked bodies
Bouddha smiles and hands talk gently to the
god of night while glowing flowers
glow in hell

Dikt
Geishas vandrar runt i
sockervärldar.
Ris faller från skyn
mot lyckliga arbetare.
Små världar utvecklas
från riset.
Blodspår efter odöda som
festat på ditt kött.

?????
Sungod on
tired windows
women carrying their babies to the
river
death waiting in line
among the washing machines
laundryroom
mongst gods and godesses
and self proclaimed
prophets

there is a God
inside of you
the silent god of all things

nostradamus
seer
of thousand eons

caught your death in midair
as if newsflash
in a magazine
and Charles Mansons cult
flashing its inherent state
of mind in my face

white hands caressing your dying flesh
searching the innards for views of the future.
Your dead words proclaiming again dead emperors.

Childless.

Död

Om man tar sitt liv, blir efterdanandet fruktansvärt för de
efterlevande.
Efterbörden-krossat ansikte, ens naglar, ens döda tunga och
ens hjärna-
skeppas omedelbart till vederbörande antika farmacist.
Ens tankar blir upphängda i taket med döda flugor.
Och ens kropp körs till första bästa kyrkogård.

Suicid är makt över de bleka gamla som måste fortsätta leva.
Gråt ej över den döde, lagd till frid i mull och jord
(som de efterlevande äter, tuggar och sväljer)
varför sörja en salig själ? (som nu sitter vid bord
med mat och vin i sina fienders åsyn)

Sörj de efterlevande. Sörj de som ska leva.

Ufos
alien dna
inside of her
and being pulled up
into a Ufo and getting
your brain sucked out
through your nose.
Their black eyes, their
hands with fingers like
spiderweb, yellow and seethrough.
They're here, and coming closer
to our planet, lifeforms and craters
of the moon. The Alien King walks
out of the UFO and listens to the signals
given to him by a King. The King sings
an opera about two siblings in greek mythology
who sleep together and the playing cards
are thrown. King wins. Alice in Wonderland
smokes pot and dances on the striped floor
with the smileycat and the Mad Hatter.
She's very happy that she's back in Wonderland
with the Queen, the Smileycat and the cards
and the roses, painted red.
A galaxy is on the screen as a screensaver
and is painted by a mad actress who visits
it she says in her dreams. A dreamworld
filled with ghosts, talking animals and a dog
with two mouths and a childlike empress.
And a deer, Frida Kahlos with the arrows.
Killer in the hotel, his ghost again vanishes
as he's pulling the body along with him.
Spiritworld and killer ants.

Missis
you've spun my head around
a tree with fabolous creatures in it,
instead of my head and someone
playing Piccola flute concert
by Vivaldi. I've cried a
river over men who didn't want me,
and those who saught my opinion
were chased away by the screaming
little creature that looks like a dog.
Two mouths and fur like spikes,
and the giant that slays those who
come close to me, is angry.
Don't come close, you only
wind up hurting me.
Don't ever love me
don't like me.
Don't be my friend,
the girl is smoking haschhisch
and carries a vanilla scenting
summersday with her.
Paradise and the man who
was turned into a woodpecker
by a witches herbs.
She is everything
he's ever wanted.
The chessgame is
ending, she won.
The chesspieces
move and walk around
on their own.
Fabolous mythological
animals are in the

paradise garden
with those funny
trees and the
man who was
turned into a donkey
by a witch.

Bouddha
A Bouddha
in a glen
in the forest,
bigger than
normal size
and made of jade.
Around it, small
lanterns glowing,
and a girl made of
Wood is praying beneath it.
The girl worships, her dark Eyes,
dark hair and wooden skin.
She sits on her knees in
indian clothing, her hands
clasped together as if in prayer.
There is a silence here but for
some flute playing from a nearby
hippie collective and the Bouddha smiles,
his Eyes shut, his gigantic hands on his knees.
The girl from the hippie collective puts flowers
there, she kneels like the wooden girl and
looks up at the Bouddha, and talks to him.
Smiling, she does meditation and says
silent prayers, and thanks him and leaves.
The flowers glow in the dark and the grass
is covered in footprints and tears.
The book of leafs is left by a pilgrim
and it lies on the ground where people
can write their poems and wishes.
Some leafs have fallen from the
tree, willow. She dares to look intó the
caleidoscope and sees patterns and

the face of Jesus.
Suddenly the sun comes down and
sings and kisses the girl.
The girl kisses the sun and
leaves with it, smiling.
The yin and yang collapse
and Bouddha opens his Eyes...

Darkness
The like
I make people unhappy
sad as it might sound.
A circus filled with
animals and
circus people
and clowns
her eyes
her thin waist
eyeliner always straight
they're standing at the pooltable
outside limelights clubs neonlights
and chinese lanterns
and a girl who looks like a moviestar
punkrock music on the stereo
and a nightopen tattoo parlour
with neonsign and a man with
brown curly hair and moustache
who does the tattooing.
He's with me, night man
who smokes marlboro
and is a gangster.
Shes burning

spontaneous human combustion
victim of a supernatural death.
She's white in the face and has
paint on it, cover of fashion magazine.
She's dead and a ghost
in the neighbourhood
pink house in the trees
garlands of faery light

Bone white structure
of his painted skullface.
African wishbones
and gatherer of
dreams. The dreameater
with his bag of dreams,
that he devours.

I'm an artstudent now.

The like.
Cats meowing in the universe.
A girl with black hair, painting,
and I love the stars, made of
plastic, that I take down from the sky
and place all over my room.
Unicorn. She's got black hair and
listens to moonmusic from some
unknown artist. Universe is a room,
with white walls and garlands of faery
light as stars. I put them on and they glow,
like diamonds. Inside the room there are
tulips in a vase and a fashion magazine.
She's laughing at neon rockstars from the
future at artworks of clouds in New York city
and crying mermaids and the conqueror
worm inside a female murder victim in an english
smalltown.

Ghosts hide in the room
as orbs, as mist or shapes
as voices, disembodied
or floating, whispering
secrets to the living.
Ghostchildren play
hide and seek, (out the door
the harmless phantom glides,)
trying to make contact with the
living, through seances, through
spiritboards. We must listen, to them
crying, talking, screaming. Children,
dead, play with toys, floating in midair.
Still the victorian ghostly mother rocks her
dead stillborn babe, and dead lovers are embraced
from hereafter. Ghosts crowd the house, the mansion,
and work there still, tending to the garden and to household
chores. One can see a candle floating in the air, in the
haunted house. One can hear them softly singing, as they
weave and sow. You can hear footsteps, or stale perfume,
when no ones there. You can see the mists, and the shape of
a man
and a woman, unlocking all the doors, making sure, making
sure.
Pictures (Victorian) of the dead, spirit photography. The mag-
azines,
with pictures of ghosts, and ghoststories. Old, decripit man-
sions,
abandoned, and vacant, with ghosts. A ghostly hand reaching
out through
a door, making contact. Flowers fading, when ghost passes
by. The

night is their time, when the victorian clock strikes twelve,
they appear.
Faded paint, old barred windows.. Skeletons, denying the fact
of bones.
Ethereal air. The spirit world around this world of sense. Hold
hands and
partake in the seance. Ghost, murdered. The closet door opens.
A ghostgirl
playing hide and seek, in my yard. Orbit of mirrors. The emp-
tiness of a mirror,
until you're not alone, and begging for release. Ghosts knock-
ing on doors,
spectral touch.

Laura
Laura Palmer dances slowly
and the dwarf sings.
The night Laura died,
a girl misscarried and
a girl painted her lips red
and the cat meowed in
the backyard. The douglas furs
blew in the wind and men who read
Lauras diary turned into rats like BOB.
The night Laura died, her friends held
a ritual in the forest. BOB and the trains
waited eerily, the scene of the murder
was still unfound by Laura and Ronette Pulaski.
the night Laura died, Donna and her
smoked cigarettes and Audrey came in
her gangstershoes to school.
Pretty but not nice. The owls were not
what they seemed and Mike, the one armed
man said fire walk with me. Two worlds.
Laura waited at the school, watched the clock,
and inside of her, the candle flickered.
The log lady hugged her log and whispered
to it, where she sat at the Diner.
The night when Laura died, the diary
was found by BOB who comes at night.
There were torn out pages and a conversation
with BOB in it. Sound of Jupiter, Lauras dead cat,
BOB took the girl, whos cat Laura hit with her car,
high on cocaine, reading porn magazines.
Shelly and Bobby were together, drinking and kissing.
The night Laura died, a girl painted her nails red
and a girl got pregnant. Laura gave the halfheart

to James.He held her, then let her go and she died.
She ran away, disappeared like a corpse candle into
the night. The street lights went to red.
Laura got home and waited for the night.
Wrote her last diary entry, and finally it came.
Her death. BOB came, and together they went
to the trains. Ronette Pulaski and Laura were
both attacked by BOB, and Laura screamed,
and she died.
Ronette Pulaski walked to town, covered in blood,
underneath her nail, B.
The morning came and Laura washed up into Twin peaks,
wrapped in plastic.

She swayed on the line, holding her umbrella. Her blue hair
burned in the moonlight. She chewed gum and her eyelids
sparkled from glitter. Her pink costume and her ballet shoes
and her leggings, all glowed like silver. Her lips were painted
with pink lipgloss and her blue eyes glowed like sapphires.
„I like walking the line, and I like the pink icecream with
sparkles.“ She walks the line, unafraid, and smiles. the crowd
cheers. The night is covered in stars, like someone pulled down
a curtain with stars on it. It shone and sparkled, the night. A
nightingale sang and some dog barked, a bulldog, and a cat
meowed. She walked the sweet grass while some bluebird sang.
She laughed and chewed her gum. Millions of stars outside
sparkled and shone like diamonds and crystals on a womans
ear. She walked inside. Her pink room was lit up by faerie lights
and her cat slept on a cushion. Jupiter it was called. She slept
on the bed, until morning. She then awoke to loud singing
outside, from a bluebird and someone was cutting the lawn.
The girl hurried to her bathroom and brushed her teeth and
put makeup on. Then she called her friend. The friend and her

decided to meet in a restaurant and discuss what they were going to do. She put her necklace on with all the spikes and she combed her hair and put the pink wig on. A picture of a Victorian lady and a nightingale was on the wall on the bathroom and a feather and some faerie pictures. She hurried out, taking her neon blue Star trek suit. Chewing her gum, she left.

Her friend with pink neon hair and her sat in the restaurant. They sat there, on a pew, drinking coke and eating burgers with french fries and dressing. Her friend wore a pink neon suit and rainbow hair. They talked about the situation of their lives, of the line dancing and the band and the poem she had written about a girl that swings in space on a swing of stars. Until the door gave way and a man walked in, with black long hair and eyeliner. And high boots. Julee looked up to her see her true love standing there, his black coat wet from the rain and his big brown eyes filled with stars and tears. Julees friend smiled at Julee, who just stared.

The hyacinths and
the jasmine trees stood
in the way of the moon.
Looking overhead, you could see
wildgeese making their way over the sky.
The house stood it's ground, and the
girl inside it, could not wait to see
the cheese moon flying about on the sky.
Lavenderscent and ambrosia, roses immortal
and water and grass, dewkissed, June night!
Her hair was tousled, and her watergrass lips
still unkissed, and her starry kiss balm eyes
were looking at father moon and stars, beaming
down on her from the sky, painted with a
pencil, made of plastic. that makes glitter
as it paints. And her cat spoke
most fervently to the moon, in it's special
cat way, before it grew wings and flew away.
She took a lock of her hair and gave it to
a faerie, who took it
to faerieland,
and showed it to the faeries-real human hair!
A nd they gathered around it and saw the lock,
and were bedazzled.
She closed the window and fell asleep
under bright beam of wings and legs from a spider,
and it's thousand eyes. Butterflies gathered
around her with auburn wings, and the sounds of
revolutionaries were heard.

She had become an angel and
given herself to God

Alla bin och blommor; farväl, älvorna flyger runt och i godtycklig förnöjsamhet skrev de pjäser och ord flög omkring dem och Louisa skrev Unga kvinnor alldeles ensam i stugan. Ihopkrupna spelade de pjäser och stampade likt elefanter. Unga kvinnor, systrar och en annan skådespelerska. Och en annan dog i gula febern, Beth. I hennes älvlika drömmar, snälla öppna fönstret sa hon. Håret förlorat, dimmig och blek och förlorad. Sjuk och borta. Det var ljuvligt att se henne komma in i paradiset. Att se henne var att älska henne. För alverna må vandra, skrev hon och morgonstjärnan ska leda oss hem. Trygg i sin hushållsblomma vilar hon med bok på blomsterbädd. Kärleken ska leda oss hem. Hennes leende ska ge oss mycket beröm och hennes pjäser ska spelas som vilken akt. Och fint och vackert är hennes anlete som vi får se. Glatt sjunger woodbirds och glad må deras sång vara. Medan hon satt i sitt rum och skrev. Thistledown! Thistledown! Här för att trösta dig är Lily Bell. Och så lämnar vi hennes ä n idag växer blomman från hennes brudklänning, så rart från hennes älskades hår.

Moon inherits
space, slowly
the sands of time
carry us towards our
Destiny. Inside of it all,
a bird is singing, a dog
is far away. A girl swings
in space, on a swing of stars.
Her Eyes are Galaxies and her
voice sings of elderly Druids,
making their way through the forest.
Her angels are watching through
burning Eyes and wings casting shadows
of stars. Their fingers are long and
their Eyes White, their skin grey and the
hair long and White. Their voices are
silky sinews of White and grey,
they cast Dreams wherever they go.
The sky is a war, between light and dark,
between night and day. The day is born,
between the bleedings legs of dawn and the
night gives Death. A Nosferatu sits infront
of a Victorian mirror, watching itself and eternity.

Nu över döda byar
nattetid, vilar den stora
månen sitt fjät och
stjärnors död
och explosion
hindrar mig från
att tänka på dig.
För du, son av
en döende dandy
och brodern till döden,
sömnen, en fallen ängel,
en nephilim. Som gör kvinnor
gravida med vampyrbarn.
Du stiger in i din svarta kappa
i dunklet av mån stjärnans sken.
Med dina ögon, dunklet av nattens
ljus, och dina läppar röda som av
blod, tar du liv. Hennes hals,
hans bitmärke. Du som försvann,
från hans födelsestad, som gick
in i skogen, för evigt. Där varulvs sonen
bor, i den dunkla skogen med hackspetten
som blev hackspett av en häxas förbannelse,
med hjortar, flöjtmusik och den söta doften
av hasch. Den lilla byn, där du föddes,
där du fanns. Du brinner likt eldarna,
du tog min hand och kysste den.
Du, som dog i sonens famn,
svartklädd och vacker,
eldstad runt din gravplats.
Som du vaknar upp från,
för att nattetid hemsöka de levande,
vampyr

Nebuktu the god of polarbears
in the Arctic, with Arctic gods
and inuits. They worship him,
go to him and pray, the polarbears,
smiling he sits there, worshipped,
the bears cry, their faces in awe
of Nebuktu. The bears stand on their
hind legs and pray, in their special
bear language, to their god.
Hindu god with two fingers up
is not as worshipped as nebuktu...
Nebuktu stands on an altar
with snow and Wood and branches.
Nebuktu is a wooden god with
painted nose, Eyes and mouth.
His blonde hair is real human hair
from a dead person and his Eyes
painted there by the polarbears.
The Life of the polarbears is
imagined by an inuit,
gods and myths.

Alice

The diamond necklace
around the cats neck in space.
Alice in Wonderland
jumps through wormholes
and finds the bunny and her sister
by the tree. The bunny says I'm
late for a meeting, and jumps down
the rabbithole and Alice follows.
In Wonderland she finds a cake.
Eat me, the cake says.
She eats it and grows small.
She is going through dimensions
and irish graves, through which
different worlds can be entered.
The smileycat disappears into the darkness in the
tree.
Alice and the smoking caterpillar smoke
and get high. Alice smiles and walks
off, still stoned, deeper into Wonderland.
The girl before the victorian dark mirror
smirks, and paints her lips black whilst her
reflection smiles.
Through the next planes, a spirit reaches
out to a seer and psychic,
a womans head in a jar is talking to her.
She saw a Titanic victim who died a death
she wouldn't wish on her worst enemy
and ghosts.
Her fun thing to do is to do spunk,
wtihout any reason. She pretends to
be a ghost to scare the mean boys away.

Dimensions away, a girl is, through different
physical planes in a dimension,
doing something completely different in
a parrallel world. She's also in the physical
plane, doing something different.

Karp

En karp på en kinesrestaurang
i ett akvarium
dagdrömmer med slöjstjärtar
anemoner och regnbågsfiskar
bland skattkistor och vackra stenar
söker efter silhuetterna
Geishor
i mångfärgade kimonos
vitmålade ansikten

kan bara drömma
där han simmar
olyckligt kär
han minns hennes ansikte
bland alla barnen
hon var speciell
inte som de andra

-inte mänsklig-
omänsklig
mytisk
magisk

han såg gälarna
han hörde hennes röst
och nu väntar han på

-återföreningen-
tills de tillsammans ska fly
demoner
andar

människoliknande
fiskvarelser

Igen
efter 1000 år
har hon inte glömt honom
bara saknat
som changelings
har de funnit varandra
igen och igen

Forest
inhale
fresh air
scent of pine and trees
green nature
holes in which Vittra hides
and the lake mirrors your
sorrows and pain...her face
in the mist. Deep inside her
where the trees are far apart.
I love the woods,
her eyes, Vittra runs
far away, luring men into the
woods, she bends down
the hole in her back
her eyes, gawking eyes of
light, her laughter.
Moon, childish in the sky
stars like a doona cover,
covering the world.
He beats the earths drum.
let me go deep into the woods
and lie down
and inhale
and be
infinite.